Generation Alpha

They're Alpha for a Reason….

Daliah Wachs, MD, FAAFP

About the Author

Daliah Wachs MD, FAAFP is a board certified family physician, nationally syndicated radio host, author and television personality.

In the 1990's she earned an Honors Degree at the University of Nevada Las Vegas and graduated Cum Laude. She attended medical school at the University of Nevada School of Medicine in Reno and trained and completed her 4th year at UCLA. She returned to Reno to graduate and then began a three year Family Medicine residency in Las Vegas, which she completed in 2000 as Chief Resident. During her residency she worked as an Emergency Room Physician in Lake Havasu, AZ and as an Urgent Care Physician in Bullhead City, AZ. She then became Board Certified in Family Medicine and immediately opened her practice in Las Vegas, Nevada. She also holds the degree of Fellow from the American Academy of Family Physicians.

Genesis Communications Network now broadcasts her show worldwide. She is heard on iHeart Radio and multiple affiliates. She has one of the fastest expanding radio shows in the world. In 2018 she made the Top 50 Radio Hosts listened to on Talk Stream Live as well as Talkers Magazine Heavy Hundred Radio Host Rankings every year since.

Dr. Daliah Wachs currently lives in Nevada where she continues to broadcast, teach, publicly speak and practice medicine.

Table of Contents

Introduction

Generation Alpha encompasses those born between the years 2010 and 2025. Hence they are still children. But don't underestimate their mark in this world.....the character of the Alphas have already begun to take shape. Although the name alpha may not be permanently used to describe their generation, Gen Alpha is being used for now and is catching steam.

Firstly, they were born after tablets and the internet became commonplace, hence their first toys were Mom's or Dad's smartphone.

They were internet celebrities before they knew it as parents blasted their pictures, including every bubble bath, poopoo diaper and first day of kindergarten all over social media. Many are more recognizable than their Baby Boomer grandparents.

Unlike their older siblings or aunts and uncles who are Millennials, they were not pushed to fast food for most meals and took on a more vegetarian diet. Come to think of it, they are the only group of children who could easily recognize tofu.

With COVID-induced fear causing parents to skip routine well checks, coupled with growing anti-vaccine sentiment, Generation Alpha may not be ubiquitously vaccinated as their other counterparts.

They may be less religious, either due to having multiple parental role models or due to COVID related restrictions on temple/church attendance, hence the future of religion is in their hands.

Alphas have also begun to not identify themselves by gender or race and have oftentimes used "restrooms" designated for any gender with ease.

Alphas are currently being trained to not use pronouns and their language is becoming devoid of archaic and politically incorrect terms used by older generations.

Many Alphas have multiple parental figures with the "nuclear family" evolving into having "sets" of mothers, fathers, grandparents and siblings.

As COVID pandemic societal changes occur, Alphas may become the generation where homeschooling and working alongside parents is the "norm", as remote employment expands and allows "work from home".

Possibly in part to their computer/tablet/phone dependency, Alphas comprise a large chunk of the myopia boom, in which record numbers of children are becoming nearsighted, requiring glasses, and later contacts or future interventions.

The Alphas will be the most expressive with their eyes and facial contortions if masks continue to be the style of the 2020s.

Hence Generation Alpha will learn they need to compete heavily for facial recognition, identity, societal value, work and family attention.

But most significantly, Alphas will be the generation least able to visualize their future careers, being less likely to tell Mom or Dad they want to become a police officer, pilot, teacher, nurse, doctor, lawyer, etc.

Alphas will therefore take on a "Wait-and-See" approach as they have learned that tech, automation, and COVID are changing the shape of education and many industries by the day.

If COVID-19 lockdowns give rise to a "Corona-baby boom", this generation could be the most populous yet.

They will want jobs, better technology and an identity other than those decade-old bubble bath photographs put on the internet years prior, however when it comes to career and housing choices, they may be less committing and more cautious and always ready for change.

So there is no doubt that Alphas will be one of the most competitive, expressive, goal oriented, compassionate, intuitive, responsible, technically savvy generations we've seen yet.

These are qualities of born leaders….hence
the name, Alphas.

Chapter 1   The Generations Before Them

The Alphas have a tough road ahead. They are born into a world occupied and molded by billions of Millenials, Generation X'ers, Baby Boomers and Traditionalists, each with their own idea of what the world should be, and whose approach is losing relevance by the day in today's ever-evolving society.

Traditionalists or the "Greatest Generation"

Known for decades as the "Silent Generation," "GI Generation," or the "Greatest Generation," those born between 1927 and 1945 have found their voice. As kids they were taught to keep their silence and let the grown ups speak but when they saw their families trudge through the great depression and WWII, they learned that they were going to have to rise and make a better world, and ironically, break free from tradition.

Although ingrained with morals, strong work ethic and following rules, traditionalists focused their strengths on creating new industries, communities with suburbs and expanded frontiers.

Traditionalist icons such Ray Charles, John Lennon, Elvis Presley, Buzz Aldrin, Neil Armstrong, Clint Eastwood and Sean Connery, for example, forever changed the world's take on music, movies and space.

The Baby Boomers

Those born between 1945 - 1960 fall under the "Boomer" category. This generation learned from their parents varying views of war and how people were treated and vowed to change and guard against oppression, mass killings, and segregation. Although initially wary, Baby Boomers began to trust technology more than their older counterparts and encouraged industries such as retail and dining to attract those who normally would sew their own clothes and cook at home to venture out and trust another's cooking, clothing and product.

They are a hard working generation but having lived under the Cold War, learned that life could be over in a second and every minute should be cherished, thus giving rise to the sexual revolution and widespread experimentation with drugs. Opposite the resolute, follow the rules, devote your life to one employer philosophy held by their older counterparts, Baby Boomers began to divorce in higher numbers and were the first generation to "live for the day."

Generation X

So by 1965 a new Generation was born. Those born between 1965 and 1980 didn't have a name, hence to this day is called Gen X.

Gen X'ers began to see a change to the nuclear family. Many with parents who divorced learned to make relationships with new maternal and paternal figures as well as siblings and roommates.

They moved often as divorces caused new residence changes and the concept of Dad or Mom having one job for 20 years didn't exist as companies would merge, become replaced or die out due to new technology.

Gen X'ers had to begin to trust a computer. A large box with a screen that had a flashing icon. They learned to trust what they couldn't see or comprehend and became one of the most open and entrusting generations.

With TV being so ubiquitous, their generation could easily see what other societies were enduring and learned that if they wanted to keep their freedom, music, jobs, style, they had to dig their heels in the ground and build a bigger and stronger country.

They built, and built, expanded and built some more, embracing the networks we were forming between new families, industries, cities and countries.

Generation X'ers therefore *connected* and became so good at connecting that they gave rise to a need to be always connected at some point. Hence the "X"………

Generation Y or Millennials

Those born after 1980 to 1995 are some of the most misunderstood on the planet. Many have accused the Millennials of being spoiled, lazy, less driven, when actually they are one of the most pivotal generations yet.

Seeing their parents become more reliant and always seeming to need to catch up on new technology, Millennials took on the role as "translator" and teacher, hence older generations such as the traditionalists and boomers found themselves relying on their grandchildren for help.

But Gen Y'ers do not have it easy. Since birth, they have been conditioned to take on the weight of an internet dependent society, with their career hopes lying in the balance of what new technology chooses when it ends one industry and opens a new one.

Their childhood hopes of having a house, solid career, and family one day seems less picturebook as the years progress.

And with automation replacing jobs and COVID era industry changes, Millennials are once again finding themselves as the buttress of society, being a source of help and solace for the other generations.

Millennials have to be creative, crafty, hard working but also practical. The old adage of needing to "own your own home" doesn't make sense to the average Millennial who sees their colleagues change jobs and cities every few years. Nor the adage of buying a new car when one loses half its value driving it off the car lot and ride sharing saves money on gas, insurance and parking.

Millennials are some of the most practical yet and teach other generations how to retrain their old school thinking.

Generation Z

Although older generations are envious of the "young and carefree" for all their access to tech and societal cushions they worked hard to build, those born after 1995 to the year 2010 feel they got the short end of the stick.

Whether it was Y2K, 9/11, the Great Recession, the Social Media explosion or COVID, Generation Z didn't know what the heck their parents were complaining about during their school days, as they are constantly being bombarded with privacy threats, responsibilities requiring connectivity at all times, and lack of direction when it came to what careers are "safe" and future goals.

They are forced to take a train that has no map or disclosure of where it is going to stop and they are not viewed upon in society as old enough to help make decisions and societal changes.

So Z'ers look to the Millenials to guide their agenda but the latter is facing their own issues with jobs, family responsibilities and keeping

Boomers and Traditionalists connected and up to speed.

So Z'ers are left with deciding if they should go to college and get a degree in an industry that may no longer exist, or choose a career that accents their strengths but is hidden by a COVID mask, or jump back on their parent's train hopefully able to continue to live with them while they are in a state of Gen. X connectivity chaos.

However their advantage is their youth, as they will be perfectly poised and able to express extreme flexibility when society and industry "resets". Lay low and loose is now their strategy.

So now we have Generation Alpha. As their older siblings, aunts and uncles begin to "lay low and loose", one would think their strategy would be the same….however they have not "laid low" as their parents have already made them internet celebrities……

Chapter 2   Celebrity Status

While Millennials and Z'ers yelled "Stop it" and "No Pics" to their older relatives fascinated with the reality of not losing precious photos or moments of life by posting every bit of life minutia from puppy pooping to their lunch choice on social media, Generation Alphas had no say.

They are too young to object and haven't learned how to isolate like teens do.

So most Alphas have been photographed, posted, commented on, shared, filtered, and enhanced on multiple IP addresses.

When they grow up and realize every moment of their infancy is a picture or video download away, some may not take it too well.

Those who choose not to identify as one gender may not wish to have previous photos expressing a wardrobe or style they would not have condoned.

In fact most of our parents dressed us in clothes we would have never chosen.

What makes the "celebrity age" of Generation Alpha more precarious is they lose their own identity to that of what their parents chose to post. A picture takes on the identity not so much of the model but of the surrounding environment, caption, lighting, and situation choreographed by the photographer.

Hence if a Generation Alpha wants to be politically neutral in life later, a picture of them wearing an election banner as a baby could mistakenly define them for life.

Hence many Alphas will have to, once they are aware, make their first goal to redefine their social media image. They may need to find their identity sooner or have a "temporary identity" such that they can erase past misconceptions.

However Alphas will be very aware, unlike Millennials whose privacy was taken away from them without warning, of how often they will be on camera.

They may be more aware of weight, style, skin care, attitude expression more than any of the previous generations.

As opposed to a background check for us older folk, an Alpha's background check will be the link population after an internet search.

They will thus become the most technically savvy generation yet…..or be the first generation to slow its roll…..

Chapter 3   Education

The Alphas didn't have a similar early education as Generation Xers, Baby Boomers or Traditionalists.

Most of us walked for miles to school with 20 pounds of books and school supplies in our backpacks, Then we sat down at a desk and stared at the teacher who would lecture at us writing with chalk, invoking giggles each time the chalk would break or the eraser would fall on the floor causing a plume of smoke.

It was all about books, researching which book, locating a book, navigating through a book, caring for a book, highlighting a book, bookmarking a page in the book, sharing a book, and closing a book.

A book elicited pride, a sense of accomplishment, a form of barter, a gift. Alphas might have played with books, but they didn't gain an appreciation for books like we all did.

Alphas never got a chance. They were first exposed to any form of education on their parent's smartphone or computer.

Whereas Millenials and Zer's watched videos and TV shows for education and entertainment, Alphas learned to stream. They spent more time focusing their developing eyes on screens than paper and TVs that were positioned feet away.

This could be the reason we are seeing such a myopia/nearsightedness boom which will be discussed later.

However schools for Alphas still incorporated group learning and hands on. Arts and crafts, sports, and circle times still persisted in weekday curriculums.

Yet more parents prior to COVID began opting for homeschool or online teaching. With school shootings, bullying and fatal food allergies, more parents found home schooling to be safer and with their child being accustomed to screen time, they opted for virtual learning options.

Now with COVID era distance learning and concerns regarding other pathogens, more parents and teachers are opting for online learning.

Crayons, pencils, scissors and sandwiches which used to be shared commonly among kids are now deemed taboo as they can hold bacteria, viruses, fungi and outright dirt.

Although some of us, including myself, predicted schools would move to online in the not too distant future due to school district struggles with budgets and finding enough educators, the COVID pandemic accelerated this move.

So Alphas may be the first generation to receive most of their childhood education online and with less social interaction.

This may augment their technical skills but what does it do to their social skills, team building, leadership expression?

Moreover many parents have a difficult time getting their child to brush their teeth let alone finish their pre-Algebra homework.

Their primary learning partner will be a parent or caregiver who has not received formal training in education. And "look it up" is not teaching.

Teaching encompasses more than just teaching a subject. It involves being a role model, mentor, adult influence, leader, supporter and one who provides a different point of view inspiring lateral thinking.

Parents do this but kids need other "teachers" in their lives.

Moreover the education one receives in school is not just math and history. They learn how to navigate around bullies, grumpy teachers, losing one's lunch money, protecting their new toy, earning respect, and gaining the attention of their teacher.

Alphas are therefore at risk of losing much of the educational opportunities given to us...much like a book......

Chapter 4   Career Choices

One might think this is an odd chapter as most children are too young to consider what type of career they will have, however most children do dream of what they will be like as a grown up and can't wait to become one.

As children, we all knew or saw someone who inspired us to become a professional and had that mental image of what we wanted to look like when we reached the right age and training.

Whether it was a construction worker, pilot, police officer, fire fighter, physician, dentist, lawyer, stock broker, chef, teacher, or clergy, the image of who we wanted to be guided us through the trials and tribulations of getting there.

The older goal-oriented generations relied on future hopes and dreams to keep them on track.

However, the Alphas don't have as clear cut a picture. In fact social media and news blurs the image of the professional they thought they wished to be. Parents may guide them into their industries, but young children finding their parents out of work or complaining about their employers and coworkers may find following in Mommy's or Daddy's footsteps unappealing.

So Alphas, just like the Gen Z's have found new types of role models. Social media/internet/podcast stars are catching their eye.

Not only are these celebrities entertaining, they also appear to be educational, hence taking on a role as teacher.

Although Zer's have the maturity to work through the content and realize three are jobs beyond broadcasting, Alphas are not meeting as many flesh and blood professionals and are predominantly being influenced by what they see online.

Hence if a post COVID era society becomes redefined by new and sprawling industries, Alphas may not have the focused image to keep them reaching for their career goal.

Older generations will tell Alphas to just stick to the books and get a degree such that when they do decide to choose a career their resume will appear to be more competitive. Yet the younger Millennials and Z'ers may differ on their opinion on degrees due to the reality of finding a post COVID era job or the practicality of a degree if one changes to pursue a different career.

So high school and higher education for Alphas may need to transition many from feeling forced to choose a single concrete degree to beginning to incorporate various online learning benchmarks that awards levels of degrees or competency certificates. Such that if a student is indecisive in pursuing a specialized degree, the average alpha student already has the necessary standard degrees to get a job in a field of their choice and can choose to move forward into more specialized education such as medical, engineering, teaching or law school for example.

And with experts predicting the Alphas may be the most populous generation yet, due to lockdowns from COVID-19, their career choice, commitment, and ability to pursue fields that need brainpower will be instrumental in maintaining future societies and economies.

Hence our job as the older generation is to encourage them to ask questions, shadow professionals to allow a peek into their industry and offer clarity when we can. If we don't, the idea of an Alpha having a fulfilling career with growth and opportunity will become extinct as career choice fails to become a goal, forcing many of them as adults to, out of desperation, choose the next available job to support themselves.

Chapter 5   Health Challenges

This is never an easy topic. Looking at a group of kids, who are bright eyed, cute and hopeful and explaining to their parents that they could face a slew of health issues if we don't intervene. Well we older generations can handle difficult subjects so let's dive right in.

Obesity

Although obesity haunts every generation, the Alphas may be at the highest risk due to their dependence on screens for education and entertainment.

Although food choices might be improving now that parents are beginning to use less soda and fast food as meal staples, kids are bombarded with advertisements online more than their parents and hence are in a position to contribute to meal choices….can even order the meal themselves using the pre populated credit card option on their parent's browser.

If home schooled or learning virtually, they are committed to keeping relatively still at a desk for hours on end whereas in a classroom setting one could fidget, get up to sharpen their pencil, move to circle time and engage in recess and physical education.

School rules of "no food in class" prevented intermeal munching. And being at school provided a much needed distraction from the smell of mom, who is also at home working remotely, prepping lunch and dinner in the background.

As positive progress has been made with bullying prevention programs and the acceptance of overweight children so as they don't feel inferior to others, the flip side is occurring as children are not being cautioned of the negative health effects due to excessive weight.

A 5 year-old child may not be convinced when they are hungry and wanting a cookie that their habits could lead to insulin resistance and a diabetic condition causing retinopathy decades from now, but they will pick up, if around other children, how the slender build might be advantageous during playground play.

Diabetes

As just discussed, obesity, lack of physical activity, poor food choices, as well as a genetic predisposition, could lead to diabetes.

Diabetes is a disease in which the body doesn't utilize and metabolize sugar properly. When we consume food, it's broken down into proteins, nutrients, fats, water, and sugar. These components are necessary for cell growth and function. They get absorbed in the small intestine and make it to the bloodstream. In order for a cell to utilize sugar, it needs the hormone insulin to help guide it in. It's similar to a key that fits in the keyhole of the "door" of

the cell, opening it up so sugar can enter.
Insulin is produced in the pancreas, an organ
that receives signals when one eats to release
insulin in preparation of the sugar load coming
down the pike.

So I imagine our mouth like a waiting room, the
blood stream like a hallway, and the cells of the
body the rooms along the hallway. Insulin is
the key to open the cells' "doors" allowing
sugar to enter. If the sugar does not get in, it
stays in the bloodstream "hallway" and doesn't
feed the cell. Weight loss occurs, and
individuals may become more thirsty as the
sugar in the blood makes it fairly osmotic,
something the body wants to neutralize,
reduce. The kidneys are going to want to
dump the excess sugar, so to do so, one would
urinate more, again causing thirst. So when a
diabetic loses weight, urinates more frequently
and becomes thirsty, you now understand why.

Uncontrolled diabetes can cause the following:

Cardiovascular disease – Sugar is sticky, so it
can easily add to atherosclerotic plaques.

Blindness – high sugar content draws in water
to neutralize and small blood vessels in the eye
can only take so much fluid before they burst.
Moreover, high blood sugar weakens blood
vessels.

Kidney disease – the kidneys work overtime to
eliminate the excess sugar. Moreover, sugar
laden blood isn't the healthiest when they
themselves need nourishment.

Infections – pathogens love sugar. It's food for them. Moreover blood laden with sugar doesn't allow immune cells to work in the most opportune environment.

Neuropathy – nerves don't receive adequate blood supply due to the diabetes-damaged blood flow and vessels, hence they become dull or hypersensitive causing diabetics to have numbness or pain.

Dementia – as with the heart and other organs, the brain needs healthy blood and flow. Diabetes has been found to increase risk of Alzheimer's as well.

So if the Alphas don't curb obesity, sugar intake, keep an active lifestyle and get regular checkups, they might face diabetes in greater numbers than the Baby Boomers.

Vaccinations/Regular Check Ups

So if getting regular checkups is key to good health, what happens in a post COVID society when family members wish to avoid medical clinics and turn to telemedicine as their primary care provider?

Well let's start by discussing what happens at a well child check.

Firstly the child meets the nurse who asks some basic medical history. Then the nurse takes vital signs including height, weight, pulse, respiratory rate, and sometimes blood pressure and pulse oximetry to check for blood oxygenation.

Then vaccine records are reviewed to see if any are due and should be given at the visit.

Then the medical provider comes in and asks more questions about current health, activity, diet, home stressors, and then performs an exam.

Scalp, skin, head, ears, eyes, nose, mouth, neck, vertebrae, heart, lungs, abdomen, extremities, posture, gait, muscle strength and neurological integrity are just a few of the body parts explored during a check up.

Then the provider gives the parent and caregiver a to-do list of what needs to be improved, provides prescriptions if needed, vaccinations if due, and commends the parents and the patient on a job well done and conveys they can't wait to see them again and see how well they're "growing".

It's a lengthy trip to the medical provider and for many, risky, as they wish to avoid other sick children or pathogens that could be lurking. So some parents have been procrastinating taking their child in.

The Alphas are therefore currently at risk of being off schedule with their vaccines and unaware if they are not "growing" properly.

Vaccines are given at the following age milestones: 2 months, 4 months, 6 months,

12-15 months, 4-6 years, 12 years, with yearly flu shots, or pre college meningitis vaccines as well.

Since virtual provider visits cannot provide vaccines, health industry leaders are discussing how to vaccinate children of families concerned to leave their house and go to a clinic.

Moreover, many children online are inundated with varying degrees of vaccine misinformation, which could contribute to their own reluctance to get the shot.

Lack of immunity to certain diseases, previously staved off by robust vaccination programs, could be problematic for our youngest generation.

And missing check ups that catch growth and development issues, could lead to a delay in intervention.

Vision issues

Over the last decade, we physicians have seen huge spikes in headaches, eye strain, and need for glasses.

Myopia, or nearsightedness, has been linked to chronic use of screen viewing. It results in images that normally could be seen at a distance to become blurry.

Glasses, contact lens and refraction surgery can assist in improving the vision. However we recommend taking frequent breaks from looking at a screen and focusing on images across the room to prevent fixed focus on a screen for hours at a time.

Online schooling may not always allow for this and should be included in any virtual curriculum.

Physical Endurance

Growing up, physical education (PE) would include learning and playing every type of sport under the sun and then running miles.

If we weren't currently commanded to run during PE, we would run at top speed to get to class after recess, or to join our friends after school, or to catch up to the bus or ice cream truck that was driving away.

The more we ran and exercised the faster and farther we could go.

Alphas who remain physically active and engage in sports and outdoor activities will most likely benefit as we did. However, if they choose to stay home, stay connected to screens and lack opportunities to join clubs or sports, their endurance, muscle strength and speed could suffer.

Sleep Issues

If you were a child who ran all day, tumbled, giggled, carried pounds of books and school supplies, argued with your siblings, and hid from mom trying to get you into a bath, chances are when bedtime hit, you were out like a light.

If Alphas run the risk of not engaging in physical activity, the natural urge to relax comes harder.

Moreover screen time can disrupt sleep and looking at the computer or tablet prior to shut eye keeps children up for hours on end.

Poor diet or eating a high carb meal before bedtime can also interfere with falling asleep.

And then smartphones or tablets beeping or turning on during the night can interrupt a restful sleep if one was fortunate enough to finally obtain one.

Therefore Alphas may be at higher risk of insomnia at an earlier age than their older counterparts.

Insomnia is a disorder where one has difficulty falling asleep and/or staying asleep. Many factors can cause insomnia. These include:

Medications (stimulants, decongestants)
Caffeine
Alcohol
Stress, anxiety, depression
Thyroid disorder
Chronic pain
Neck and back arthritis
Diabetes
Respiratory conditions (asthma, COPD)

Gastroesophageal reflux
Urinary frequency
Diarrhea
Neurological conditions
Sleep apnea

and of course environmental issues such as noise, temperature, and pets jumping on the bed.

Treating insomnia can be complex. We begin by treating the underlying cause, such as any of those listed above. Then we can try the following:

- Lowering the room temperature to an average of 65 degrees F
- Shut off artificial lights 1-2 hours before going to bed
- Avoiding alcohol in adults and teens
- Dinner including foods rich in tryptophan (fish, nuts, tofu, turkey, eggs and seeds)
- Warm bath
- Cognitive and/or behavioral therapy
- Aromatherapy including lavender
- Black out curtains to keep out light
- Daily exercise

to name a few.

Sleep is very crucial to the developing brain and allows "body repair" to occur. Those who are sleep deprived may suffer from health conditions such as obesity and diabetes, as well as depression.

Depression

Childhood depression occurs more often than we realize. Although genetics, diet, lack of physical activity, sleep, and bullying can contribute greatly, screen dependence is also a risk factor.

Signs of depression include:

- insomnia
- fatigue
- wanting to avoid others
- poor appetite
- lack of sex drive
- apathy
- anxiety
- sadness
- tearful
- mood swings
- poor memory
- poor concentration
- overeating

and more…..

So we as parents and providers look for these symptoms and try to intervene early one.

Alphas, if they don't have good eating, exercise, screen and sleep habits, are at high risk of depression.

Chapter 6 Political Correctness

So what are Alphas in a good position for? Well many won't make the same mistake their older generations have when it comes to using archaic terms or phrases which no longer are deemed acceptable.

For those of us who were punished in school everytime we used a plural pronoun to describe a singular person, as in the sentence, "The teacher called Johnny in class; he stood up (as opposed to they stood up)", we struggle to break away from the years of singular pronoun ingraining and ruler slaps to our wrists.

Alphas, however, are in a perfect position to learn the new vernacular without having the confusion of having learned it another way years prior.

Moreover, attitudes towards other genders, races, abilities and challenges have been taught to this generation from the beginning to be kind, accepting and non-offensive.

Whereas in previous generations a statement such as "You have a fantastic body!" would range anywhere from being a complement to being harassing in nature, Alphas will already know what may not be acceptable to say and have learned predefined phrases that hopefully won't get them into trouble in their adulthood.

And if the rules change, as these things do evolve in society, the Alphas are in a great position to adapt as they have learned since childhood that what may be acceptable today may not be acceptable tomorrow.....a concept difficult for the less flexible and regimented older generations.

Chapter 7   Skepticism vs. Religion

All of us as children were conditioned to not believe everything we hear.

As we got older we were encouraged to research and verify things we couldn't understand. Finding the sources, studies, evidence, or experts could be tricky and time consuming. And we had to choose if it was worth putting the time and work into it, or taking the information at "face value."

By the time the internet pervaded our lives, however, we had information, studies, "evidence", at our fingertips, twenty four hours a day, seven days a week.

Opinions shared cyberspace with references and many of us older folk began citing "facts" which were actually "opinions" made to look like facts.

Generation Alpha, therefore, has been trained from the beginning to be wary of "news".

Fact checking and taking into account the source became vital to verifying if the type of news or information being posted was able to be considered "fact" or "opinion."

So while the older generations were instructed as kids to not question authority, the Alphas are forced to question internet "authorities" on a regular basis.

This generation will most likely combine efforts with the Gen Z and Millenials to cyberly define "fact" from "fiction", separating sources as were done in our school libraries.

However, older generations may become frustrated with the Alpha's skepticism. The latter in turn may appear unruly and defiant, causing a huge generation gap.

If a child has been exposed to so many "facts" that turn out to lead them down the wrong reference path, they will be less likely to take an older person's "word for it."

However, many of them may be less likely to get duped. Patterns of fake social media profiles, sponsored content, and opinions posing as facts will be easily discerned by this adeptly scrutinizing generation.

Social media predators who were easily able to fool all generations in the newly formed cybersphere, will be less likely to convince the Alphas to "meet them for lunch". However, we must expect they will create craftier ways to lure unsuspecting fawn and need to be prepared for those.

Which brings us to religion. Many wonder if the Alphas will be less spiritual than others?

The older, regimented generations such as Traditionalists and Baby Boomers were used to rules and following them. When questions or clarification was sought, as children they were told to "not ask questions" and "just believe."

Alphas will not be a generation that is comfortable with "just believing" as they've been ingrained to research everything they read and hear.

So parents and clergy will need to continue to offer open discussions about religion to entice the younger generation to remain engaged during religious discussions or prayer.

If social distancing and places of worship restrictions stay in place due to COVID or other pandemics, attendance will drop. Although religion will still be taught in the home, Sunday School, church functions, temple services, and activities that engage children and young adults, may not be as robust as they once were leading to less church memberships and religious community engagement.

Additionally with spirituality, many older generations believe they saw the work of the Lord visually, reporting sightings of Holy figures, or witnessing supernatural acts such as seeing a family member recover when they were on the brink of death.

Younger generations, however, have been so hyperstimulated by computer generated imagery seen in games, movies and at concerts that they may be numb to what older generations would describe as spiritual "signs."

So there is not doubt that the Alphas have the potential to become a less religious generation. And their ingrained skepticism will be a challenge for those older teachers, employers and even clergy who wish to guide them.

Chapter 8   Family Dynamics

The Alphas are still young and not thinking about having a family for the next few years. However their current family dynamic may shape their own family dynamic and is worth exploring.

Some Alphas enjoy the "nuclear family" with both parents and siblings living together. Others enjoy the love of multiple parents having step parents, or significant others of their parents, providing care, support and affection. Some Alphas may also be cared for by their grandparents as the Great Recession and then COVID induced recession made living with grandparents more financially feasible for their parents.

Generation Alpha are also becoming accustomed to a world where children do not necessarily need to have a mother AND a father.

Surrogates and adoption allow same sex couples to have children and build a "nuclear family."

While the Millenials and Gen Z'ers saw a trend in high divorce rates, Alphas may see divorce rates stave off as fewer couples choose marriage.

Unlike the older generations who kept to the tradition of meeting someone, falling in love, marrying them and staying married to them until "death do us part", the younger generations such as Millenials and Gen Zs questioned the practicality of forming a legal union with someone whom you could later fall out of love with and want to divorce.

So Alphas will balance the traditions and romantic concepts of finding and dedicating one's life to their betrothed to the practicality of living with someone they care for and with which they've had a child.

But if the Alphas become more dependent on the internet and screen time for their education, social interaction and work, they may face obstacles when engaging in physical relationships.

The Alphas therefore risk being one of the least social generations.

However, they may be the most evolved when it comes to expressing feelings.

Mask and social distancing, used ubiquitously during the COVID and post COVID pandemic, have caused people to find new ways to communicate.

Alphas will most likely have an easier time than their older counterparts, adapting to become more animated with their facial expressions that are hidden by a face covering developing more social tools and expressions of emotion than ever before.

Alphas will also evolve into not needing as much physical contact to learn of the other person's feelings which could make them much more sensitive and "in tune."

So later, the young adults of Generation Alpha might be the ones pivotal in steering the post-COVID dating and family dynamics.

Chapter 9   Competitive But Cautious

The Alphas will soon become adults and storm the workforce before we know it.

They will face fierce competition like no other generation before them.

Whereas young adults for years surpassed older individuals in being tech savvy, most of the Baby Boomers and Gen X'ers will have caught up with their computer skills in order to keep their jobs.

Moreover, being more youthful and energetic, once pluses in a brick and mortar business that required person-to-person contact, may now be less valuable when remote sales and virtual commerce pervade many industries.

Hence the young Alpha adults can't bank on their youth and computer skills to outperform an older, more experienced, competitor.

Moreover jobs that do rely on automation will continue to expand while the humans who become replaced add to the growing population of job seekers.

So Alphas will face more competition than any other generation in their age group.

Some might encourage those in Generation Alpha to get a degree, but with online schooling and calls for free college for all increasing access, degrees may not stand out as they once did, deterring one from making the multiple year commitment.

Moreover as industries die from automation and post COVID era changes and some evolve due to technology, a current Alpha's career may not have even been invented yet.

So the Alphas, at their very young age, will learn to be patient. They watched Generation X and Millennials commit years to an industry that later changed to an unrecognizable form, or obtained an expensive degree that ended up never being used. So they will need to be the most strategic planning their next steps.

Some might find the trade industries such as plumbing, electrical, welding, etc. be under sought and find a career path that is the road less travelled.

Others may find the pendulum swing so far in either direction that jobs in finance, medicine, and retail will once again want people to take over what computers apathetically controlled, making college degrees more enticing once again.

And Generation Alpha, if deterred by initial competition for their career choice, may choose to initially focus their post high school efforts on military service, volunteering or leisure.

But make no mistake, the Alphas will be ready.

They've been reading, watching and studying all of us older generations online, an exposure the average child growing up in older generations did not have.

At a young age Generation Alpha learned to critique news, opinion, and internet spam all while honing skills in technology, online relationships and mask-hidden facial communication.

Not being committed to "learning the family business", Alphas have learned that they have choices and actually lots of them.

As with all the generations before them, they will be stereotyped and criticized for having lack of direction, social interactions and commitment.

But like all generations before them, they too will be underestimated, and when they are allowed to surface and shine as adults, they will contribute and reshape the world at a speed and determination never seen before.

They are, after all, the Alphas…..

www.ingramcontent.com/pod-product-compliance
Lightning Source LLC
Chambersburg PA
CBHW051127250726
48655CB00007B/2928